Tramps in the Kingdom

Tramps in the Kingdom

by

Iain Reid

drawn by

Fiddy

HODDER AND STOUGHTON
LONDON SYDNEY AUCKLAND TORONTO

British Library Cataloguing in Publication Data

Reid, Iain
Tramps in the kingdom.
1. Christian life – Caricatures and cartoons
I. Title
741.5'942 PN6737

ISBN 0 340 23947 6

First published 1979

Printed in Great Britain for
Hodder and Stoughton Limited,
Mill Road, Dunton Green, Sevenoaks, Kent
by Hazell Watson & Viney Ltd, Aylesbury, Bucks

Introduction

When I first tried to get my Tramps strip published, back in 1966, I could not find an editor who was interested. Dejected, I tore up the strips but, almost without my knowing it, the idea continued to simmer away in my mind and to develop in my subconscious. This went on for ten years and, as it grew, it changed.

My original ambition had simply been to produce a funny stripcartoon. The ten years' enforced gestation period, however, added a new dimension. When, in 1976, I decided to have another go at Tramps, I still wanted it to be a funny strip, but I wanted it also to say something about life and death and all stations in between.

This, I think, is the added ingredient which turned a failure into a success. The *Daily Express* took the plunge on September 6 and were soon followed by the *Sunday Express*. Response was immediate and favourable. Percival and Cedric quickly won a place in the hearts of millions of readers, one of whom actually sent me two luncheon vouchers to buy them a decent meal!

Whoever wrote the book of Ecclesiastes certainly knew a thing or two when he said that there is a time to be born. I now see that it is lucky for me that the Tramps did not make their entry into the world prematurely.

One day, soon after the series started, my Tramps went to church. They sat alone. No one spoke to them. They heard fine words extolling love, generosity and compassion, yet they went on their way still hungry. Sunday after Sunday, they discovered that some of us who call ourselves Christian fall short of the mark. We fail to practise what we preach.

Fortunately, their unhappy experiences did not demoralise the Tramps. Undeterred, they continued to go about their business exemplifying those very qualities which they did not always find in church – kindness, humility, love, concern, faith, generosity, forgiveness. Because they owned nothing and had no material gods to worship, Percival and Cedric were liberated from the world's net. They were free to be human, free to inherit the Kingdom.

As time went by, the Tramps took on a life of their own. They became almost independent of me. As they grew and developed inside me, all I had to do was to tune into their conversations. Fiddy, who draws the strip so well, also found out that Percival and Cedric began to change visually as he got to know them better. This is why I have decided to publish the strips in this book in strict chronological order – to allow for this natural development.

I am sometimes asked what is the intention behind the so-called 'religious' episodes of Tramps. The answer is that, among other things, I am trying to show up some of the imperfections of organised religion in this era of spiritual dryness.

But why, as a regular and committed churchgoer, do I allow my Tramps to uncover the skeletons in our cupboard? Why do I bring them face to face with the church's weak points all the time instead of introducing them to its enduring strengths? Well, sometimes one must be cruel to be kind. My criticisms are meant to be constructive.

Only by acknowledging its shortcomings, and doing something about them, will the church, in my view, attract the great wide world into its fellowship. Only by looking honestly at itself, will the church discover those flaws and imperfections which prove a barrier to its work of bringing men and women to an awareness of the presence of God.

The Archbishop of Canterbury, Dr. Donald Coggan, pointed to some of these imperfections at the 1978 Lambeth Conference when he preached to 400 plus bishops from all over the world. Courageously, he said that some of them had given up believing that God still speaks to the church.

He added, 'God forgive us. We would not admit it; it would shock our congregations if we did. But we have stopped listening, and our spiritual life has died on us, though we keep up appearances and go through the motions.'

If the Archbishop of Canterbury can look at the church through truth-tinted spectacles, why shouldn't the Tramps?

IAIN REID

AHEM!

HAVEN'T WE FORGOTTEN SOMETHING, CEDRIC?
?

FOR WHAT WE ARE ABOUT TO RECEIVE...
10
FIDDY

WE ARE NOT AS OTHER MEN, I AGREE, CEDRIC—AND SOME MAY CALL US **LAYABOUTS**

BUT WHEN, AT LAST, OUR SOULS STAND BEFORE GOD, WE WILL BE **INDISTINGUISHABLE** FROM OUR FELLOW MEN
FIDDY

WON'T THE **SMELL** GIVE US AWAY?

CONSIDER THE LILIES OF THE FIELD, CEDRIC, THEY TOIL NOT NEITHER DO THEY SPIN...

YET EVEN SOLOMON IN ALL HIS GLORY WAS NOT ARRAYED LIKE ONE OF THESE
FIDDY

THAT'S GOOD STUFF, PERCIVAL. ***WRITE IT DOWN BEFORE YOU FORGET IT***

TUT-TUT, CEDRIC. WE MUST NEVER ASK GOD FOR MONEY

RATHER WE SHOULD ASK GOD FOR THE STRENGTH TO ACCEPT, UNCOMPLAININGLY, OUR IMPOVERISHED CONDITION
FIDDY

32
WHO DO WE ASK FOR MONEY THEN?

THE CHURCH WAS **CROWDED** TODAY, PERCIVAL

INDEED IT WAS, CEDRIC...

YET IT WAS SURPRISINGLY EMPTY WHERE **WE** WERE SITTING!
38
J FIDDY

FATE MAY NOT HAVE DEALT US A VERY GOOD HAND IN THIS LIFE, CEDRIC...

BUT IF, AS OUR BUDDHIST FRIENDS BELIEVE, THERE ARE LIVES TO COME...

...I MAY BE REINCARNATED AS A MAN OF SUBSTANCE. YOU MIGHT EVEN BE THE *POPE*!

TEACH YOURSELF ITALIAN
42
FIDDY

THANK YOU
FIDDY

OUR SITUATION, DEAR CEDRIC, IS NOT DISSIMILAR TO THAT OF THE MAN IN THE BIBLE STORY WHO WAS ATTACKED BY ROBBERS...

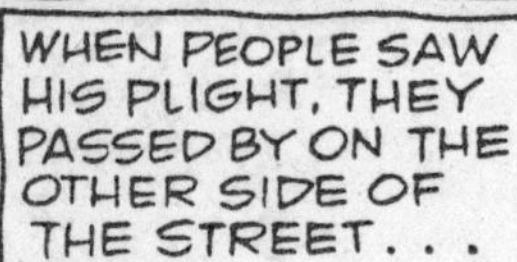

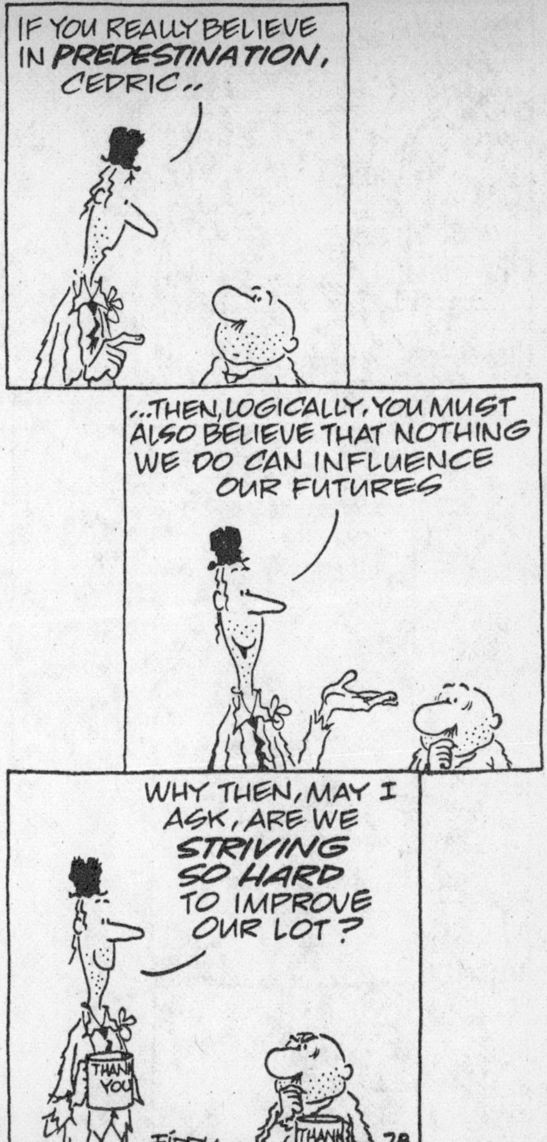

WHY THEN, MAY I ASK, ARE WE **STRIVING SO HARD** TO IMPROVE OUR LOT?

FIDRY

78

WHY DOESN'T ANYBODY EVER SPEAK TO US AT CHURCH, PERCIVAL?

NOW, NOW, CEDRIC! HAVE YOU FORGOTTEN THE ELDERLY LADY WITH THE FUR COAT? **SHE** ONCE SPOKE TO US

SHE TOLD US THAT THE LIKES OF US SHOULDN'T BE ALLOWED IN!
FIDDY

IF, AT THIS PRECISE MOMENT, DEATH WERE TO LAY HIS ICY HAND UPON YOUR SHOULDER, CEDRIC...
...WHAT DO YOU SUPPOSE YOU WOULD SAY TO HIM?
WHAT KEPT YOU?
FIDDY
87

NOW THAT CHRISTMAS IS ALMOST UPON US, CEDRIC, WE MUST PREPARE OURSELVES FOR MUCH BIGGER TAKINGS
THANK YOU
THANK YOU
THANK YOU
THANK YOU
92
FIDDY
ONCE OUR FELLOW HUMANS BECOME INFECTED WITH THE CHRISTMAS SPIRIT, THERE WILL BE NO BOUNDS TO THEIR GENEROSITY
I AM BEGINNING TO AGREE, CEDRIC—THIS YEAR THEY APPEAR TO BE IMMUNE TO INFECTION

AND NOW, CEDRIC, WE APPROACH THE PEAK, THE ZENITH, OF OUR YULETIDE MERRIMENT

MAY I SUGGEST THAT WE DO NOT PULL TOO HARD TOO QUICKLY?

93
GOOD IDEA, PERCIVAL- LET'S MAKE IT LAST!
FIDDY

TRULY YOU HAVE
NO CAUSE
TO COMPLAIN,
CEDRIC...

YOU LOST
FAIRLY AND
SQUARELY ON
THE SPIN OF
A COIN

94
NEXT CHRISTMAS, IT WILL
BE *MY* TURN TO HAVE
FROZEN FEET
FIDDY

BLEST ARE THOSE WHO KNOW THAT THEY ARE POOR— THE KINGDOM OF HEAVEN IS THEIRS
105

YIPPEE!
FIDDY

...THY KINGDOM COME..

...THY WILL BE DONE ON EARTH AS IT IS IN HEAVEN...

GIVE US THIS DAY OUR DAILY BREAD

WILL WE KNOW EACH OTHER IN THE LIFE TO COME, PERCIVAL?
FIDDY
I HOPE SO, CEDRIC, UNLESS, OF COURSE, ONE OF US GOES TO HEAVEN AND ONE GOES TO THE OTHER PLACE!
BUT WE'RE MATES, PERCIVAL! SURELY THEY WOULDN'T SPLIT US UP!
124

WHATEVER YOUR NEEDS MAY BE, SIMPLY TRUST IN THE LORD...

...HE WILL PROVIDE
FIDDY

CLINK!
CLINK!
RATTLE!
RATTLE!

THE LAST THING I WISH TO BE IS AN ALARMIST, CEDRIC

I DO, HOWEVER, ENTERTAIN GRAVE DOUBTS CONCERNING OUR ABILITY TO WITHSTAND THIS SUB-ZERO TEMPERATURE

GOODNIGHT, OLD CHAP— SEE YOU ON THE OTHER SIDE
132
FIDDY

MORNING HAS BROKEN, CEDRIC, AND, MUCH TO MY SURPRISE, WE HAVE SURVIVED THE COLDEST NIGHT OF THE YEAR

AND HERE COMES BIG NELLIE WITH A JUG OF STEAMING TEA AND BISCUITS

OH, DEAR, I FEAR WE HAVE NOT SURVIVED AFTER ALL! I RATHER THINK THIS MUST BE *HEAVEN*
FIDDY

DON'T FORGET, SIR, IT IS EASIER FOR A CAMEL TO GO THROUGH THE EYE OF A NEEDLE...
FIDDY

...THAN FOR A **RICH** MAN TO ENTER HEAVEN
THANK YOU

WELL, DON'T BLAME **US** IF YOU'RE NOT ALLOWED IN!
THANK YOU

I CANNOT UNDERSTAND IT, CEDRIC. THE CHURCH SERVICE SHOULD HAVE ENDED TEN MINUTES AGO!

OH, DEAR! I THINK THEY MUST HAVE SPOTTED US...

THE VICAR'S SAID PRAYERS FOR THE QUEEN, THE PRIME MINISTER, TRADES UNION LEADERS, DOCTORS, NURSES,,,

...BUT NOT A WORD ABOUT THE LIKES OF US WITH NO ROOF OVER OUR HEADS!

147
PATIENCE, CEDRIC, PERHAPS WE'LL COME UP UNDER *ANY OTHER BUSINESS*!
FIDDY

I VERY NEARLY ENTERED A MONASTERY WHEN I WAS A YOUNG MAN, CEDRIC
THANK YOU
BUT I SIMPLY COULD NOT BRING MYSELF TO TAKE THEIR VOW OF POVERTY
THANK YOU
IRONIC, ISN'T IT?
THANK YOU
FIDDY

IT WAS MOST KIND OF THE VICAR TO ASK US TO TAKE UP THE OFFERING, CEDRIC

HE MUST TRUST US, PERCIVAL
INDEED HE DOES, CEDRIC

159
THE *FRISKING* WAS EXTREMELY HALF-HEARTED!
FIDDY

THANK YOU, MADAM. I AM TOUCHED BY YOUR GENEROSITY

WE MUST REMEMBER THAT DEAR, COMPASSIONATE WOMAN IN OUR PRAYERS TONIGHT, CEDRIC
165

FIDDY

IT IS TRULY REMARKABLE, CEDRIC! LAST NIGHT I PRAYED FOR PIE, CHIPS AND PEAS...

...AND TODAY, WHAT DO WE HAVE?
PIE, CHIPS AND PEAS!
FIDDY

...ONE RARE, ONE MEDIUM, AND TO FOLLOW WE WILL HAVE ***PEAR BELLE HÉLÈNE,*** IF YOU PLEASE
MENU

PERCIVAL
YES, CEDRIC

WHY CAN'T THE VICAR DRESS ORDINARY...

...JUST LIKE YOU AND ME?
FIDDY
177

WHAT SHALL YOU AND I SAY TO OUR MAKER, CEDRIC...
...ON THAT DAY WHEN WE STAND BEFORE THE JUDGMENT SEAT ACCUSED OF HAVING WASTED OUR LIVES?
183
NOT GUILTY, YOUR HONOUR
FIDDY

ACCORDING TO ASTROLOGY, CEDRIC, OUR FATE IS DETERMINED BY THE POSITION OF THE STARS AT OUR BIRTH

FIDDY

PERCIVAL!
YES, CEDRIC?

YOU KNOW THAT STORY ABOUT JESUS FEEDING 5000 PEOPLE WITH ONLY FIVE LOAVES AND TWO FISHES?

188
ANY IDEA HOW IT'S DONE?
FIDDY

YOU AND I, CEDRIC, ARE MERELY DRIFTING THROUGH LIFE
YOU'RE RIGHT, PERCIVAL

LET US SIT DOWN AND MAKE SOME PLANS FOR THE FUTURE

FIRST OF ALL, WHICH HYMNS WOULD YOU LIKE AT YOUR FUNERAL?
FIDDY

YOU PROMISED IN YOUR SERMON THAT WHEN WE GO TO HEAVEN WE WON'T BE HUNGRY OR THIRSTY ANY MORE

THAT IS QUITE CORRECT

CAN I HAVE IT IN *WRITING*, PLEASE?
194
FIDDY

WHAT A DIFFERENCE A SPOT OF SUN MAKES TO ONE'S MORALE, CEDRIC
FIDDY

IT LIGHTS UP THE DARK CORNERS OF ONE'S SOUL. IT CHASES AWAY ONE'S GLOOMY DOUBTS. IT FILLS ONE'S HEART WITH HOPE...

199
IT DRIES OUT YOUR CLOTHES

... AND YOU ARE ALL INVITED TO JOIN US FOR COFFEE AND FELLOWSHIP AFTER THE SERVICE
FIDDY

TO MINGLE WITH ONE'S FELLOW-CHURCHMEN, CEDRIC—WHAT JOY IT IS!
200

YOU DON'T **HAVE** TO GO TO CHURCH TO SEEK HELP FROM GOD, CEDRIC

GOD IS **EVERYWHERE**- IT IS JUST A QUESTION OF FINDING HIM

COME OUT, COME OUT, WHEREVER YOU ARE!
205
FIDDY

ALL THINGS BRIGHT
AND BEAUTIFUL
ALL CREATURES
GREAT AND...

...SMALL
206
FIDDY

AHH, CEDRIC, WE ARE SAVED. HERE COMES A REVEREND GENTLEMAN OUT FOR HIS AFTERNOON WALK
FIDDY

EXCUSE ME, SIR, NEITHER FOOD NOR DRINK HAS PASSED OUR LIPS SINCE WEDNESDAY
RUMBLE

HIS MIND IS ON **HIGHER** THINGS, CEDRIC
RUMBLE

SIR THOMAS FONSONBY, CAPTAIN OF INDUSTRY, CHAIRMAN OF THREE MAJOR COMPANIES, DIRECTOR OF SIX OTHERS...
FIDDY

A MULTI-MILLIONAIRE WHOSE EVERY WAKING HOUR IS SPENT TOILING AT HIS DESK

THERE, BUT FOR THE GRACE OF GOD, GO I

YOU MAY HAVE NOTICED, SIR, THAT MY FRIEND KEPT NODDING OFF DURING YOUR SERMON ON BROTHERLY LOVE —
FIDDY
I AM ANXIOUS TO ASSURE YOU THAT HE INTENDED NO DISRESPECT
IT IS SIMPLY THAT, **NOT HAVING EATEN FOR THREE DAYS**, EXHAUSTION OVERCAME HIM
218
THAT'S QUITE ALL RIGHT. NO OFFENCE TAKEN!

HOW ARE YOU FEELING NOW, CEDRIC?
JUST THE SAME!
FIDDY

HAVE YOU BEEN PRAYING CONSTANTLY TO BE HEALED?

YES, PERCIVAL... BUT I DON'T THINK HE'S IN!
224

CONSIDER THIS FLOWER, CEDRIC. LIKE US, IT DOES NO WORK, YET GOD GIVES IT ALL THE SUSTENANCE IT REQUIRES
FIDDY

NOW, DOES NOT THAT TELL YOU SOMETHING ABOUT GOD?

230
YES—HE PREFERS **FLOWERS**!

WHEN I WAS A BOY, I DREAMED OF PUTTING THE WORLD TO RIGHTS, CEDRIC

I HAD A VISION OF A WORLD WITHOUT SICKNESS, PAIN OR SORROW...

...A WORLD FULL OF HAPPY SMILING FACES

I'VE *FAILED!*
FIDDY

IF ONE HAS FAITH, CEDRIC, ONE NEED HAVE NO FEAR OF DEATH

IT IS SIMPLY LIKE GOING ON A LONG JOURNEY

YES! BUT WITH A ONE-WAY TICKET!
FIDDY

TUT-TUT, CEDRIC. TRY TO KEEP YOUR MIND OFF FOOD. PRAY FOR SPIRITUAL GIFTS
242
FIDDY

PRAY TO BECOME A FINER PERSON, TO HAVE A NOBLER CHARACTER

...AND PLEASE GIVE ME HUMILITY AND CHIPS PATIENCE AND CHIPS KINDNESS AND CHIPS

PRAYER, CEDRIC, IS THE INVISIBLE TELEPHONE WHICH CONNECTS MAN TO GOD
FIDDY

HELLO! HELLO! HELLO!

248
NO REPLY!

THAT WAS A
MAGNIFICENT
SERMON ON
THE JOY OF
BEING A
CHRISTIAN

BUT, TELL ME,
CEDRIC, DID
ANYTHING
ABOUT THE
PREACHER
STRIKE YOU?
YES...

...HE NEVER
SMILED
ONCE!
PRECISELY!
FIDDY
254

DEATH, CEDRIC, IS NOT SOMETHING TO BE **FEARED**
FIDDY

DEATH IS THE **DOOR** THROUGH WHICH WE PASS TO THE ETERNAL LIFE BEYOND

IF YOU GO FIRST, PERCIVAL, PROMISE YOU'LL **SHUT** THE DOOR BEHIND YOU!
260

I BELIEVE THAT
EVERYTHING WE DO
IS NOTED UP THERE,
CEDRIC...

THIS LIFE IS, AS IT
WERE, AN EXAMINATION
AN
EXAMINATION?

266
AND I BET I
KNOW WHO
COMES
BOTTOM!
FIDDY

ON SUCH A DAY AS THIS, CEDRIC, ONE IS TEMPTED TO DANCE THROUGH THE STREETS SHOUTING...

...GOD'S IN HIS HEAVEN, ALL'S RIGHT WITH THE WORLD!

ONE **DOESN'T**, OF COURSE, HAVING BEEN LET DOWN SO OFTEN!
FIDDY

COUGH!
COUGH!
COUGH!
COUGH!
COUGH!
COUGH!
I THINK WE HAD BETTER LEAVE, CEDRIC...

COUGH!
COUGH!
COUGH!
COUGH!
COUGH!
YOU ARE KEEPING THE CONGREGATION AWAKE!
FIDDY

WE THANK YOU FOR YOUR BOUNTIFUL GIFTS...

...AND WE PRAY FOR THOSE WHO ARE LESS FORTUNATE THAN US

...WHO ARE **EVEN** LESS FORTUNATE THAN US, HE MEANS!
FIDDY

CEDRIC, GO AND INVITE HARRY AND BIG NELLIE TO SHARE OUR GREAT GOOD FORTUNE
FIDDY

FOR WHAT WE ARE ABOUT TO RECEIVE...

AMEN!
AMEN!

AHEM ... CEDRIC! EVERYONE IS LOOKING AT YOU!

284
NO SMILING IN CHURCH!
FIDDY

FETE
CHURCH FETE
IN AID OF THE CHURCH RESTORATION FUND
OUR BRIEF APPEARANCE AT THE CHURCH FETE, CEDRIC, WILL GLADDEN THE HEARTS OF THE ORGANISERS

FETE
THEY WILL BE ABSOLUTELY DELIGHTED TO SEE US GO!
HOME MADE JAM AND CHUTNEY
CAKES BUNS BISCUITS
WHITE ELEPHANT STALL
FIDDY

THE VICAR SAID THAT, INSTEAD OF PRAYING FOR OURSELVES, WE SHOULD PRAY FOR OTHERS...
FIDDY

SO TONIGHT, I WILL PRAY FOR YOU, CEDRIC
AND I'LL PRAY FOR YOU, PERCIVAL

AND WE'LL GO HALVES, OKAY?
290

I AM AFRAID THAT YOU ARE WASTING YOUR TIME PRAYING FOR FINANCIAL HELP, CEDRIC

GOD DOES NOT **HAVE** ANY MONEY

296
OH, NO! DON'T TELL ME **HE'S** BROKE TOO!
FIDDY

ONWARD CHRISTIAN SOLDIERS,
MARCHING AS TO WAR...

302
FIDDY

UNFORTUNATELY, WE NEED £20,000 FOR THE RESTORATION OF THE BUILDING, £25,000 FOR A NEW ORGAN, £100 FOR CHOIR ROBES...

PLEASE BE FAIR, CEDRIC...
MUMBLE! MUMBLE! MUMBLE!

...HE WAS KIND ENOUGH TO EXPLAIN **WHY** HE COULD NOT SPARE US THE PRICE OF A CUP OF TEA!
308
FIDDY

DO NOT LAMENT OUR EARTHLY POVERTY, CEDRIC
MAN DOES NOT LIVE BY BREAD ALONE

WE DO!
FIDDY

OUR ORGAN HAS BROKEN DOWN, BUT WE ARE FORTUNATE IN HAVING A VIOLINIST IN OUR MIDST WHO HAS KINDLY AGREED TO ACCOMPANY OUR HYMN-SINGING
FIDDY
CEDRIC!

314
SORRY, PERCIVAL... FORCE OF HABIT!
THANK YOU

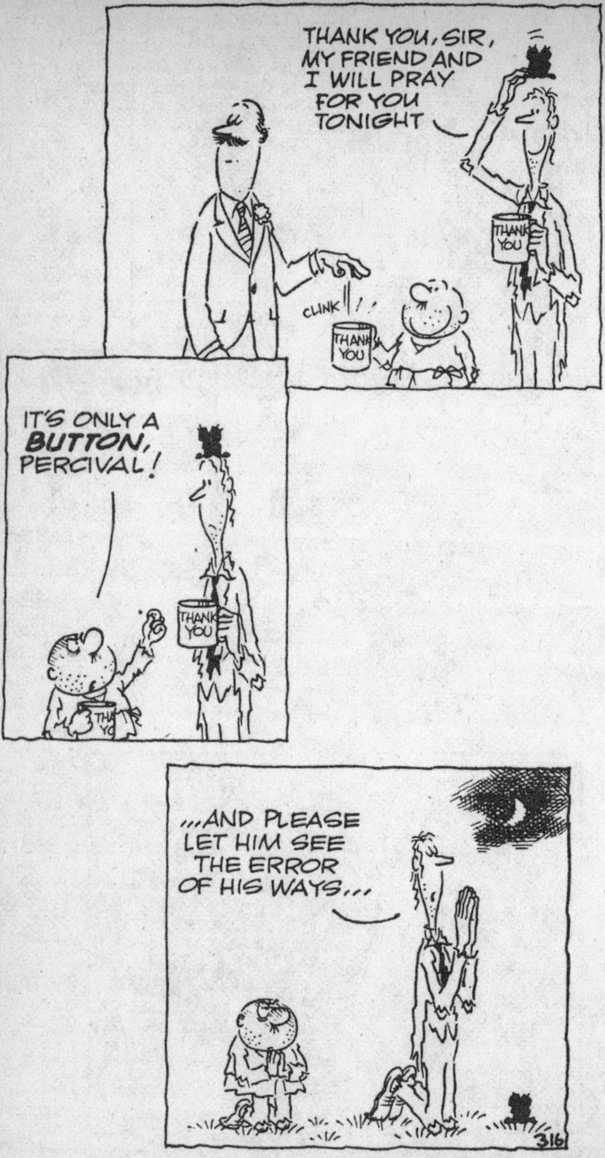

THANK YOU, SIR, MY FRIEND AND I WILL PRAY FOR YOU TONIGHT

CLINK

THANK YOU

IT'S ONLY A **BUTTON**, PERCIVAL!

THANK YOU

LOVE YOUR ENEMIES...
THAT IS CHRIST'S
COMMANDMENT TO
YOU AND TO ME
FIDDY

?
?

KEEP THINKING,
CEDRIC...
SURELY WE
MUST HAVE
SOME
ENEMIES!
320

I GOT SHOES...
...YOU GOT SHOES...
...ALL GOD'S CHILDREN GOT SHOES
326
FIDDY

ST. MARY'S PAROCHIAL COUNCIL MET ON TUESDAY AND DECIDED TO MAKE YOU A SMALL DONATION...
FIDDY

...ON **ONE** **CONDITION**
?
?

FAREWELL, ST. MARYS... **ST. MARGARETS**, HERE WE COME!
332

GOD ALWAYS ANSWERS OUR PRAYERS— SOMETIMES HE SAYS "YES", SOMETIMES HE SAYS "NO"
I FOUND THAT SERMON EXTREMELY ENCOURAGING, CEDRIC
SO DID I, PERCIVAL

350
SOMETIMES GOD SAYS YES!
FIDDY

HOW ARE YOU FEELING TODAY, CEDRIC?
A LITTLE BETTER THANKS, PERCIVAL

COULD YOU MANAGE SOMETHING TO EAT— SAY A LITTLE CLEAR SOUP AND SOME CHICKEN?
YES, I THINK SO, PERCIVAL

356
PLEASE, GOD, LET CEDRIC HAVE A LITTLE CLEAR SOUP AND SOME CHICKEN
FIDDY

Y-Y-YOU'RE W-W-WASTING YOUR T-T-TIME THANKING G-G-GOD FOR ALL OUR B-B BLESSINGS, PERCIVAL
FIDDY

H-H-HE'LL N-N-NEVER M-MAKE OUT WH-WHAT YOU'RE S-S-SAYING
WH-WHY N-N-NOT, CEDRIC?

B-B-BECAUSE YOUR T-TEETH ARE CHA-CHA-CHATTERING!
CHA CHA CHA

362

WHEN, AT LAST, YOU AND I HAVE SHUFFLED OFF THIS MORTAL COIL, CEDRIC...
R.I.P.
Sacred to the Memory of
FIDDY
...WILL ANYONE REGRET OUR PASSING?
367
I WILL!

G-G-GOOD
N-N-NIGHT,
P-PERCIVAL
G-G-GOOD
N-N-NIGHT,
CEDRIC
FIDDY

S-S-SEE
YOU IN THE
M-M-MORNING

373
IN TH-THIS
W-WORLD
OR THE
N-N-NEXT!

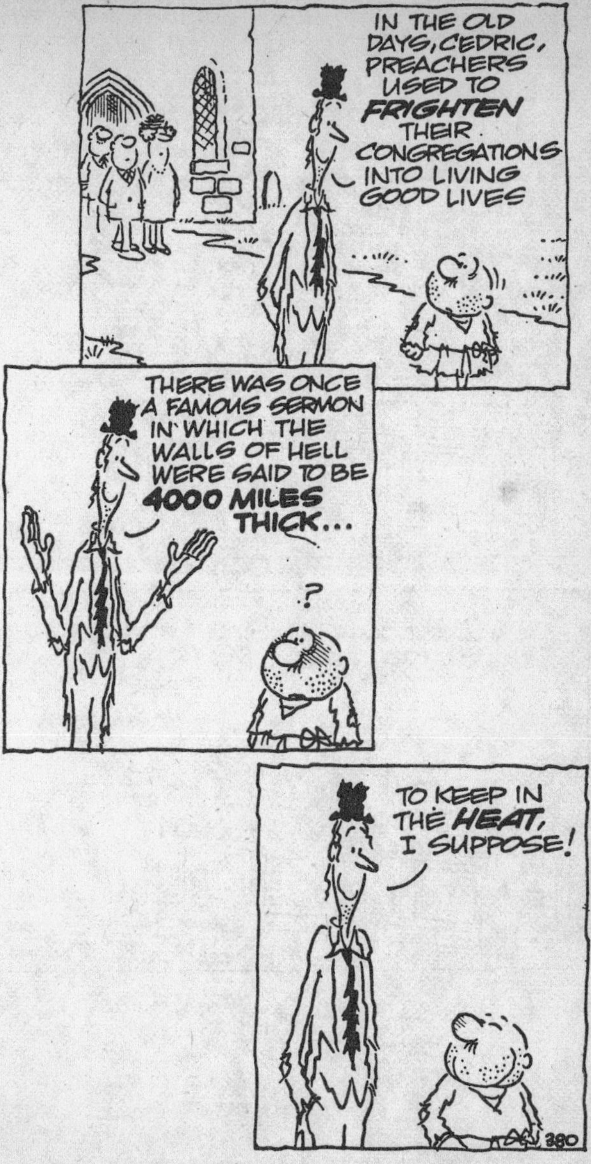

IN THE OLD DAYS, CEDRIC, PREACHERS USED TO ***FRIGHTEN*** THEIR CONGREGATIONS INTO LIVING GOOD LIVES

THERE WAS ONCE A FAMOUS SERMON IN WHICH THE WALLS OF HELL WERE SAID TO BE **4000 MILES** THICK...

?

OUR COLLECTION
LAST SUNDAY
AMOUNTED TO
SIXTY-FOUR POUNDS,
THIRTY-TWO PENCE...

... AND TWO
BUTTONS!
FIDDY

FIDDY

WHAT IS THE MATTER, CEDRIC? YOU HAVE GONE AS WHITE AS A SHEET

I HAD A PENNY AND A BUTTON IN MY POCKET...

386
...AND I'VE STILL GOT THE BUTTON!

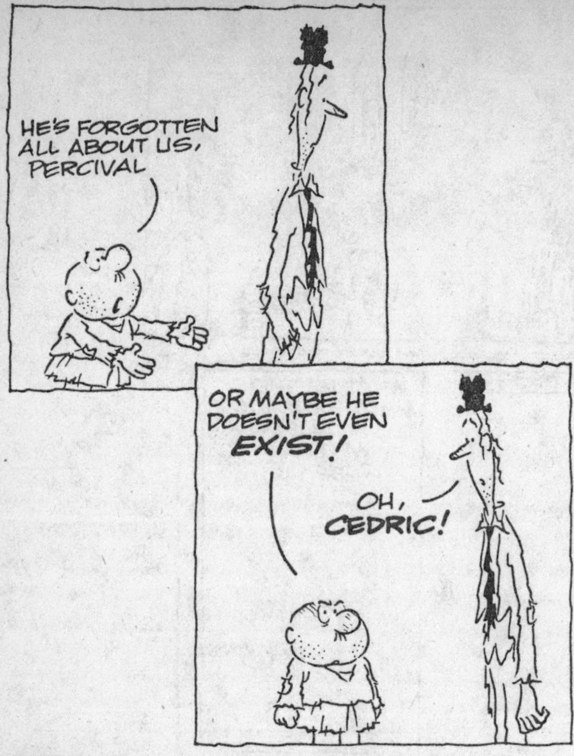

HE'S FORGOTTEN ALL ABOUT US, PERCIVAL

OR MAYBE HE DOESN'T EVEN **EXIST!**

OH, **CEDRIC!**

WHEN, ON JUDGMENT DAY, CEDRIC, IT IS POINTED OUT THAT YOU AND I SELDOM DID ANYONE A **GOOD TURN** HERE ON EARTH...
FIDDY

...WHAT WILL YOUR EXCUSE BE?

396
GOOD TURNS COST **MONEY**!

LET US PRAY, CEDRIC, FOR THOSE MILLIONS OF ENSLAVED MEN AND WOMEN...

...WHO ARE LOCKED UP IN OFFICES FIVE DAYS A WEEK FROM 10 O'CLOCK TO 5·30

LET US PRAY THAT THEY DO NOT FORGET THE LIKES OF YOU AND ME!
THANK YOU
THANK YOU
398
FIDDY

A SPOT OF CHABLIS FOR ME...
AND SOME CIDER FOR ME

YOU SEE, CEDRIC, THE GOOD LORD PROVIDES EVEN FOR THE LIKES OF US!

CHEERS!
CHEERS!
400
FIDDY

IF YOU CAN STAY FOR COFFEE AND FELLOWSHIP, WILL YOU PLEASE ENTER THE CHURCH HALL BY THE DOOR ON MY LEFT

A NOMINAL PRICE OF **THREEPENCE** PER CUP WILL BE CHARGED

413
FIDDY

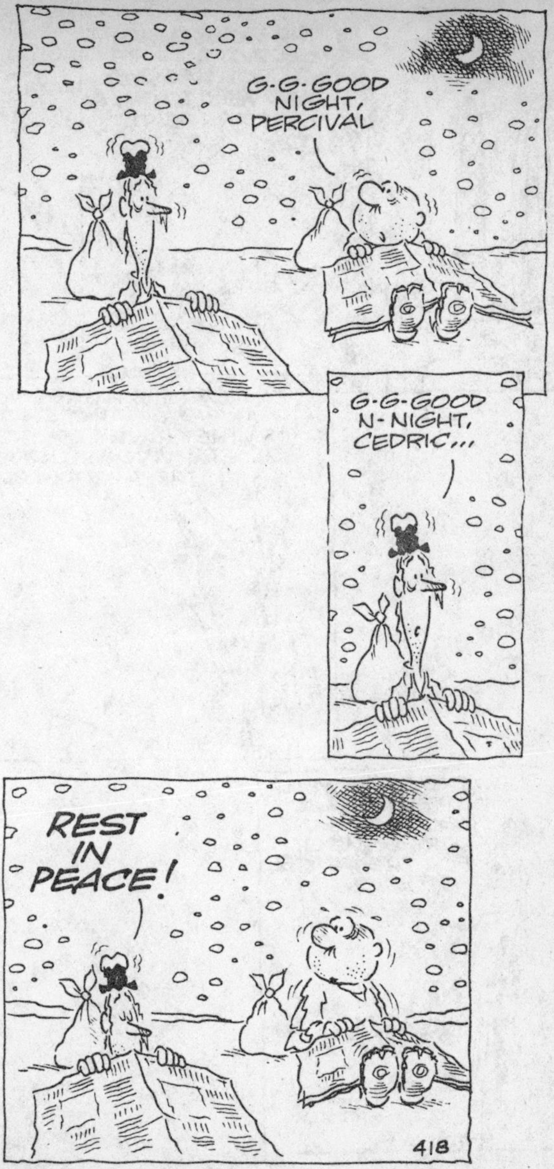

G-G-GOOD NIGHT, PERCIVAL

G-G-GOOD N-NIGHT, CEDRIC...

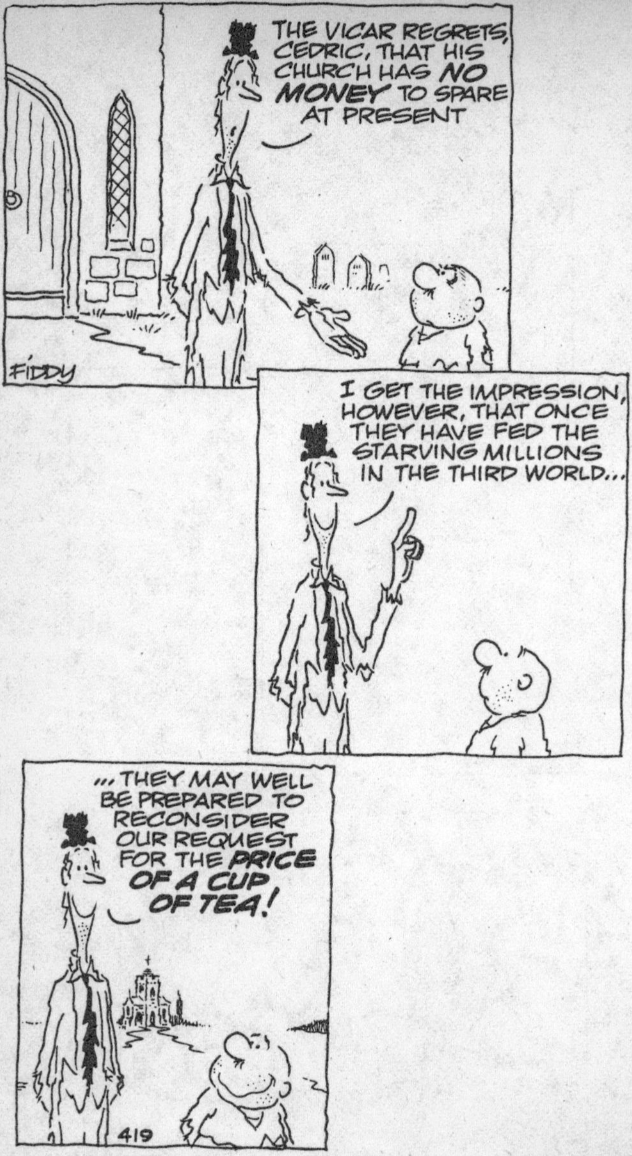

THE VICAR REGRETS, CEDRIC, THAT HIS CHURCH HAS **NO MONEY** TO SPARE AT PRESENT

FIDDY

I GET THE IMPRESSION, HOWEVER, THAT ONCE THEY HAVE FED THE STARVING MILLIONS IN THE THIRD WORLD...

DEAR GOD...

...PLEASE LET IT STOP **RAINING**

RESTAURANT
MENU
EXCUSE ME, YOUR REVERENCE...
I WOULDN'T TRY AND EAT HERE IF I WERE YOU
WHY EVER NOT?

THEY DON'T LET YOU IN WITHOUT A *TIE!*

CEDRIC...
FIDDY

YES, PERCIVAL?
JOG
JOG
JOG
JOG

DO WE REALLY *WANT* TO LIVE LONGER?
?
JOG
JOG
JOG
430

DEAR GOD, IT'S ME AGAIN...
FIDDY

PLEASE MAKE ME KIND AND GENEROUS...

...AND GIVE ME SOMETHING TO BE GENEROUS *WITH*!

CEDRIC, YOU HAVE FORGOTTEN TO SAY YOUR PRAYERS
FIDDY

NO I HAVEN'T, PERCIVAL

I DECIDED TO GIVE GOD A *NIGHT OFF!*

CEDRIC
YES, PERCIVAL
THE END OF THE WORLD IS NIGH
PREPARE TO MEET YOUR DOOM
FIDDY

IF THERE IS ANY TRUTH IN THESE PRONOUNCEMENTS,,,
THE END

,,, PERHAPS WE OUGHT TO HAVE ASKED FOR PAYMENT IN ADVANCE!
432

GOD IS LOVE... GOD IS THE GROUND OF OUR BEING... GOD IS THE IMMOVABLE MOVER...
WELL DONE, CEDRIC– YOU ARE LEARNING QUICKLY!
EASY THEOLOGY
FIDDY

NOW, HAVE YOU ANY FURTHER QUESTIONS ABOUT GOD?

437
YES, PERCIVAL... WHAT COLOUR IS HIS BEARD?
EASY THEOLOGY

DEAR ME, CEDRIC,
YOU HAVE REALLY
BLOTTED YOUR
COPYBOOK THIS
TIME...

WHEN ONE AGREES WITH
A PREACHER, ONE MAY
DEMONSTRATE ONE'S
ACQUIESCENCE WITH
A GENTEEL NOD OF
THE HEAD OR AN
APPROVING
SMILE

BUT ONE NEVER
NEVER NEVER
SHOUTS
"HEAR
HEAR"!
FIDDY

THERE IS A SAYING, CEDRIC, THAT IT IS WRONG TO LOOK FOR GOD, AND WRONG NOT TO LOOK FOR HIM
FIDDY

HOW DOES ONE RESOLVE SUCH A DILEMMA?
EASY!

HEADS WE LOOK FOR HIM, TAILS WE DON'T!
443

I COULD NOT BUT NOTICE THAT NEITHER OF YOU PUT ANYTHING IN THE COLLECTION PLATE THIS MORNING
FIDDY

WE CANNOT DENY IT, SIR. MY FRIEND AND I ARE— HOW SHALL I PUT IT— TEMPORARILY EMBARRASSED!

449
WE'RE ALWAYS TEMPORARILY EMBARRASSED
THANK YOU

YAWN!
WHERE ARE YOU GOING, PERCIVAL?

TO HAVE MY AFTER-LUNCH NAP, CEDRIC

OH... IS IT THAT TIME ALREADY?
YAWN!
FIDDY

AND NOW I WOULD LIKE YOU ALL TO SHAKE HANDS WITH YOUR NEIGHBOURS . . .
?
?
FIDDY

455

CHEER UP, CEDRIC! JUST BECAUSE WE ARE POOR AND STARVING TODAY...

...IT DOES NOT FOLLOW THAT WE SHALL BE POOR AND STARVING IN THREE MONTHS' TIME

WE MAY, BY THEN, HAVE **FORSAKEN** THIS VALE OF TEARS!
R.I.P.
458

DEAR GOD, AS YOU KNOW, PERCIVAL AND I GO TO CHURCH EVERY SUNDAY...
FIDDY

...AND WE SAY OUR PRAYERS NIGHT AND MORNING AND READ THE BIBLE QUITE A LOT...

IS IT **TOO MUCH** TO EXPECT A LITTLE SOMETHING IN RETURN?

IF THIS WEATHER CONTINUES, AND WE ARE UNABLE TO PROCURE FOOD AND SHELTER, I DO NOT HONESTLY GIVE MUCH FOR OUR CHANCES
OH, DEAR,...
FIDDY 461

...BUT THANK YOU FOR LETTING ME KNOW...

WE SHALL QUITE UNDERSTAND IF WE DO NOT SEE YOU NEXT WEEK

ALL THE MONEY I TAKE TODAY, WE SHALL GIVE TO THE CHURCH. AGREED, CEDRIC?
S'POSE SO!
THANK YOU
THANK YOU
FIDDY

BLESS MY SOUL, CEDRIC... MY CUP OVERFLOWETH
AND MINE IS EMPTY!
THANK YOU

I RATHER THINK THAT WE HAVE PROVED CONCLUSIVELY THE EXISTENCE OF GOD!

AND FINALLY, LORD, WE PRAY FOR THOSE WHO ARE HUNGRY, AND ASK THAT YOU WILL FEED THEM

467
AMEN
AMEN
AMEN
AMEN
FIDDY

CEDRIC, LET US OPEN THE GOOD BOOK AT RANDOM...
THANK YOU
FIDDY

PERHAPS, THERE, WE SHALL FIND A MESSAGE OF HOPE WHICH WILL RAISE UP OUR DOWNCAST SPIRITS
FLICK

473
MY SERVANTS SHALL EAT BUT YOU SHALL STARVE; MY SERVANTS SHALL DRINK BUT YOU SHALL GO THIRSTY
THANK YOU

...AND WE PRAY THAT THOSE WHO ARE OUT OF WORK MAY SOON FIND EMPLOYMENT...
FIDDY

I AGREE, CEDRIC, IT IS VERY WORRYING INDEED,. ESPECIALLY AS WE MUST BE ABOUT DUE TO HAVE A PRAYER ANSWERED

THE LAW OF AVERAGES, YOU KNOW!

... WE DO NOT ASK FOR **RICHES**, GOD... ONLY FOR SUFFICIENT MONEY TO KEEP BODY AND SOUL TOGETHER
FIDDY

?
?

... WITHOUT ACTUALLY HAVING TO **WORK** FOR IT!
484

I WONDER WHAT WOULD HAPPEN, CEDRIC...
FIDDY

...IF, INSTEAD OF SAYING "GIVE US THIS DAY OUR DAILY BREAD," WE SAID...

..."GIVE US THIS DAY OUR DAILY LANCASHIRE HOT POT?"

AND WAS THERE ANYTHING ABOUT THE SERMON WHICH PARTICULARLY APPEALED TO YOU TODAY, CEDRIC?
FIDDY

YES, PERCIVAL...

IT WAS **SHORTER** THAN USUAL!
490

BUT WHAT IF THERE'S NO LIFE AFTER DEATH, PERCIVAL?

IN THAT CASE, CEDRIC, WE WILL SIMPLY SLEEP ETERNITY AWAY

GREAT! I ENJOY A GOOD KIP!
496
FIDDY

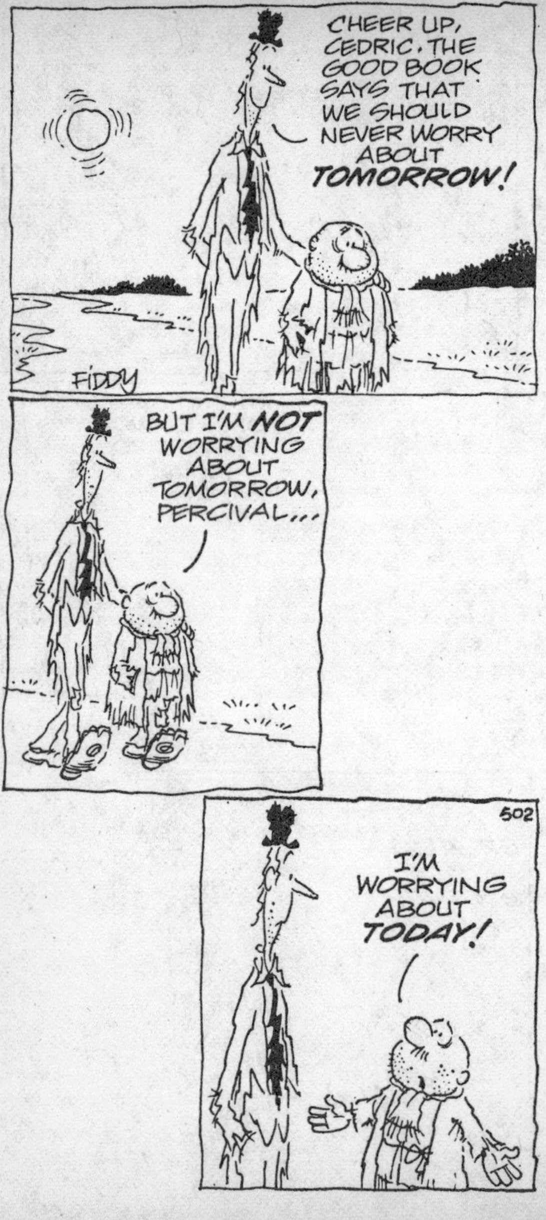

CHEER UP, CEDRIC. THE GOOD BOOK SAYS THAT WE SHOULD NEVER WORRY ABOUT **TOMORROW**!

FIDDY

BUT I'M **NOT** WORRYING ABOUT TOMORROW, PERCIVAL...

I WONDER HOW JESUS MANAGED TO TURN WATER INTO WINE, PERCIVAL?
FIDDY

UNDOUBTEDLY, THROUGH THE POWER OF PRAYER, CEDRIC
PRAYER?

PERCIVAL... WHITE OR RED?
506

DO YOU EVER FEEL, CEDRIC, THAT LIFE IS HARDLY WORTH LIVING...
?
FIDDY

...THAT NO MATTER HOW HARD ONE STRIVES, FATE HAS GOT IT IN FOR ONE?
?

ONLY WHEN I'M HUNGRY...

... WHICH IS ALWAYS!
511

TUT-TUT, CEDRIC,...
THANK YOU
FIDDY

...HAVE YOU FORGOTTEN WHAT IT SAYS IN THE GOOD BOOK?

SIX DAYS SHALT THOU LABOUR AND DO ALL THY WORK!

I WAS WONDERING...
UNITED REFORMED CHURCH EWELL
FIDDY

WOULD EITHER OF YOU GENTLEMEN CARE TO READ THE LESSON NEXT SUNDAY?

513
HOW MUCH DO YOU PAY?

NOW, TO PROVE THAT WE HAVE FAITH THAT GOD WILL **PROVIDE**, CEDRIC, LET US PUT ON THE FRYING PAN
FIDDY

AH! HERE COMES BIG NELLIE!

BETTER MAKE THAT **THREE** SAUSAGES!

AND, FINALLY, GOD, PLEASE MAKE US KIND AND FORGIVING...
FIDDY

...HELP US TO BE COMPASSIONATE LOVING AND MERCIFUL

AND WE WOULDN'T SAY NO TO A BITE TO EAT!

DING
DONG
DING
DONG
WHEN WE HAVE FINISHED BELLRINGING, CEDRIC, I RATHER THINK THAT THE VICAR INTENDS TO GIVE US A MEAL
FIDDY

YOU CAN HAVE MINE, PERCIVAL

I'M AIR-SICK!

PLEASE BLESS CEDRIC AND HELP HIM TO FIND A JOB
!
FIDDY

AND PLEASE BLESS PERCIVAL AND HELP *HIM* TO FIND A JOB

TWO CAN PLAY AT *THAT* GAME!

IT'S A LOVELY MORNING, PERCIVAL. WHAT DO YOU WANT TO DO TODAY?
FIDDY

LET US SIMPLY GO WHERE THE SPIRIT **MOVES** US, CEDRIC!
GOOD IDEA!

Z Z Z Z Z Z Z
Z Z Z Z Z Z
530